THE MAN SOCIETY DEMANDS

By Lincoln E. Anderson

The Man Society Demands Copyright © 2020 by Lincoln E. Anderson.
Lincoln E. Anderson all rights reserved Self Published
kingdomillumination@gmail.com.

This is a work of fiction. Any names, places, events or characters are only the figment of the authors imagination or used fictitiously.
ISBN: 978-1-736-85660-4
Printed in the United States of America.

All rights are reserved. No part of this novel may be reproduced, stored in or introduced into a retrieval system, or transmitted in any form without prior permission from the owner/publisher.

Dedication

This book is dedicated to my wife LaToya; my apple of gold in pictures of silver. She is my lover, partner and true wind beneath my wings. I also dedicate this book to my three beautiful children LaTasha, LaTesha and Lincoln II.

Acknowledgements

Writing a book was a dream that seized my mind and wouldn't allow me to rest until I submitted to do it. Being a son, father, brother, cousin and uncle in a family of dreamers, I wanted to be an achiever at something. I found myself feeling the pressure while reading the story of Joseph in the Bible. Knowing it was only by the grace of the Creator that my eyes were being enlightened, I wanted to pen some of the pains and joys of our society.

The first person I would like to thank is my one and only mother, Ms. Bobbie Jean Anderson Boddie. I also give great honor and respect to my father, Simon Reeves and my sweet stepmother, Beatrice Reeves. I offer a special thanks to my dear and beloved siblings starting with the late Chriss Tine Reeves, the late Priscilla Ann Boddie, (with many tears), Willie C. Reeves, Bernice Willis, Leila Martin, Roxie Moton, Tony Reeves, Bruce Anderson, Curtis Boddie, Eric Boddie, John Reeves and Casey Reeves.

I give special thanks to the With One Accord Church family and friends. I would feel out of sorts if I did not pay homage to the late, most honorable, Archbishop Apostle Horace Leonard for encouraging me and bringing me to, Triumph.

I thank the Miracle Deliverance Church family for receiving me out of the streets and washing me with God's word, and His loving kindness. Thanks to Pastor Lydia Syed and the Grace and Deliverance Church family.

To Apostles Wayne and Deborah Shepphard of Unveiling Words and the congregation. I speak on behalf of myself and my family when I say how truly humbled and blessed, we feel being able to spend time worshiping and fellowshipping under the example of your guidance and leadership.
With sincere expression of our appreciation and gratitude, we thank you.

Lincoln E. Anderson

Foreword

by Fredrick R. Bailey

As I was sitting in my apartment watching one of my favorite television shows, The Golden Girls, my cell phone began to vibrate. To my joyful surprise it was my father calling. I answered the phone and began talking to him. As the conversation went on, he reminded me to send him another copy of my book since he'd given his copy to an associate. He wanted to read, yet again, about the hardships I faced due to his absence in my life. By this point, I was all ears and eager to hear his next words.

He continued by apologizing for the pain and hurt I had to endure. I would be dishonest if I told you, I didn't feel some comfort in these words because surely, I did. However, my father's words did not bring me much closure, and not for lack of care or love for him, but because I had accepted his apology years ago. As a teenager, forgiving my father brought true healing and closure. But somehow, I felt his atonement was much more sincere. To be honest, I had learned and understood that if my father never apologized, I would have been okay. That's because I am responsible for my own joy and happiness. See, I didn't need this apology from my father. I am who I am because of those tough times. When I was just a young child, my parents were caught in the grips of drugs and alcohol. I was forced to suffer as a result of their bad habits. There were times when the electricity was turned off and sleeping through the summer heat or awaking to a freezing room in the middle of winter was my reality. Running water was often not available and food was scarce. Living in homes infested with rats and roaches was the norm. I went to five different elementary schools and struggled with reading, writing and understanding new concepts. I believe this is what he wanted to read about again.

With God, I've accomplished so much that I wouldn't have the imagination I have without the kind of childhood I had to face. So often we try to compare our lives to others, completely unaware that this is not healthy for us. We are who we are because of our past experiences and we should accept every situation and learn from them. With that being said, I love my father. And, I know he did the best that he knew how. I believe the apology was intended for his own healing and I love that he is growing and making better decisions.

In this book, Lincoln first paints a picture of a young man growing up without his father and falling victim to deeply negative influences. This young man focused his energy on young ladies and making "easy money." Was it because his father wasn't around? And if fathers are present, does this mean poor decision-making will be less likely to happen? What about the role of other prominent male figures?

I encourage you to continue reading and discover Lincoln's unique views on the matter. It doesn't matter what limitations you have in life or who was present or absent; it's all about the choices we make. We have the power to ensure that we are living the best life we possibly can. Yes, it will be challenging at times, but it is possible to succeed. While reading this book, you will come to realize that true success comes when God, the creator of the universe, constitutes the center of your life, your decisions and your actions. Lincoln is a living testimony of that. As he walks you through his past promoting the good and teaching about the bad, you will find that he has a heart for God that is pure and devoted. He serves Him and inspires others through his writing and personal lifestyle to do the same. This book is a must read. Of that, there are no doubts.

Before delving into Lincoln Anderson's groundbreaking book, "The Man Society Demands", I would like to share a poem that seems appropriate.

When you go through worried trials,

Broken hearts and pretend smiles,

Just look above and ask the Lord

How much, this pain, can I afford?

God knows how much is enough for you,

He needs to get His message through,

He wants you to call on His precious name,

God will reward you with love and fame.

If you have troubles anywhere

God wants to hear from you in prayer,

Just ask of Him what you must do

For He is love, and God loves you.

-Mae Futter Stein-

Contents

PART I

1
Valuable Demands...1

2
Demand Awakened...15

3
A Mother's Love..21

4
Man Brings Forth a Child..27

5
City Life Spoiling..37

6
A Fatherless Son Reunited..45

PART II

7
Life Demands Initiation. 49

8
A Loveless Generation. 55

9
The Emptiness Syndrome. 59

10
Live Your Life 65

11
Societal Suicide by Reason. 69

12
If a Man Loves a Woman..77

13
When Stake is Higher than Demand. 91

14
Aftermath of a Drug War 95

15
The Demand on My Life 103

PART I

1
Valuable Demands

Waking up each morning, he prays unto God. He begs God to forgive him of his innumerable sins – even those he has yet to commit. He then begs God to forgive his debtors which are also many. Later, after communing with God, he reads the Word for personal encouragement. Upon greeting his wife and children, his virtue begins to flow from within as he listens to and attends to their desires for attention and substance.

The one thing that drives him and brings him happiness with each passing day is a sustained commitment to his personal constitution. It is a part of the ledger written in permanent ink on his heart after having endured so many trials and tribulations in his lifetime.

Constantly being reminded of his past, he never forsakes his mannerisms, his temperament or the love and peace he received from his mother. She had told him numerous times of his being denied by his biological father before birth. And this left a permanent scar on his heart. He was a young, broken man. She was freshly out of a broken relationship that simply couldn't survive the free love and sexual deviance of the 1960s.

A particular lesson she reminded him of day after day was to live a life of respect, "for respect is earned and not given." This was her mantra. Her teaching him to cook, clean, iron and sew early in life was to make him a most valuable player. She knew all the players whom she had played so well. Specifically, she knew they lacked game and didn't have an adequate plan of action. Determined that her baby boy would not become another victim of such a cruel society, she taught him to not depend on the acceptance and appreciation of the rest. Little did he know that at the age of 18, he would be faced with the same pressing situations she had warned him about.

His dilemma began in the 1980s when Michael Jackson was still thrilling and Prince was raining purple. Hardcore hip-hop was bringing noise and pain to all reaches of society. As a weekend clubber and avid follower of all the hottest DJs, young Joshua knew they would bring the girls out. One DJ he really liked would sing out the names of each girl and when they heard their name being called out while dancing erotically, it made him desire more than just a dance. The amatory expression he saw in those females drove him to a compromising position, causing him to forsake his mother's persistent lecturing. He thought a lot about her sobering admonition and, after seeing these girls shake and quake week after week, he knew there had to be more to this sex life than just playing and laying. Through the smoky, low-lit nightclub, he saw their desire for intimate companionship and attention.

About a month after having glued his eyes on the prettiest girl he'd ever seen, and knowing with certainty she was looking back at that same moment, he presented to her a proposition she just couldn't resist. It made this young lady want him, just as she longed to hear her name being called out by the DJ. The constant sexual attention she received from Joshua, led her to distance herself from the idea of a meaningful relationship, especially given that her boyfriend was off at college and out of sight. Once Joshua realized the attraction was mutual, the intimacy began to flow. In fact, it flowed so richly that he ended up losing his mind in her comfort.

It was through this encounter that a baby was conceived. As this was his first true sexual relationship, he didn't have the slightest idea of how to handle the situation. His emotions were raging. And with it being her first pregnancy, compounded by morning sickness and being unsure which of her two men fathered the baby, she ultimately claimed it was the college boy's.

But with sorrow in her heart, she felt and knew almost without a doubt that it was Joshua's baby. All he knew, on the other hand, was that he enjoyed the thrill of being with her without any consequences for his actions. Even still, he was genuinely heartbroken over the fact that he had made such an extraordinary investment and would receive no credit for the miracle that was to come. When the baby was born, he ran back to her, seeking yet another opportunity to use his smooth charm and wit to convince her to be with him. But his attempt was short-lived as he realized she was not playing around. Her decision, as it seemed, was final, even as people remarked how much the baby looked like him. She was sticking to her guns on this one.

However, the rumor mill churned as the child grew up. Joshua had finally convinced her that he was truly okay with her decision in accepting that the baby was not his and that he would take no part in its life. So, as time passed, he once again found himself working on developing his sex life into something more. "She's hearing me, but she's not feeling me," he would often think to himself. It was at this point that Joshua made the decision to accept the rejection without showing her his hurt feelings. He would continue holding himself together in her presence, but away he felt that another baby boy had been abandoned.

One evening after work, she gave in to his undying efforts to get it on again after weeks of his trying to convince her. But afterwards, they both went their separate ways; he could never get over the hurt and rejection he felt from that moment. It just wasn't the same and he knew it never would be again.

The pains of ole he had felt in his mother's heart were now running rampant in his own. He tried to self-medicate the pain and became a hustler; a small-time gangster in his town. All this did was multiply the troubles in the life of a young fool trying to make a name for himself.

Occasionally, he would still go to the clubs, but his interest in seeing the girls, showing love and cutting up was fading fast. His mind was fixed on making money and raising hell.

As he continued with his self-destructive lifestyle, his family tried convincing him to get a job and steer clear of trouble. But they didn't understand the fierce hardships and pains that controlled his soul. He, however, already knew that history was repeating itself; he saw it before his very eyes. The memory of a conversation he'd had with his beloved mother drove him to drinking as he made an audacious attempt to shadow his secrets. His mother had told him of painful thoughts of carrying him nine months, all the while knowing there was to be no father present to share the joy and pain of bringing him forth. Still, she always made a point to let him know that he was loved and appreciated.

Joshua was ashamed and embarrassed, mostly due to the open rejection he had received as of late. Many others knew he had been in this relationship and the vast majority of them knew how it ended too. As they say, news travels fast, be it by telegram, phone or word of mouth.

Even though he wasn't in the child's life whatsoever, he would constantly hear people say that he had a son who looks and acts just like him. People truly believed he was the daddy and it was these encounters that led him to a greater conviction of what society thought about a bastard child and a good-for-nothing burnout father like himself. He remembers his mother saying constantly, "Just because others act a fool don't mean you have to act a fool as well." She knew good and well that he was getting into something that was not good for him, but she couldn't quite put her finger on it.

Then one day, while washing his laundry, she came across a small, cellophane bag containing a white, powdery substance. She had never seen anything like it before in his pockets but she knew exactly what she was dealing with. Waiting for the opportune moment to share her unfortunate discovery, she kindly asked him to come to the utility room. Upon his crossing the doorway, she reached over to the shelf to grab the bag and held it out for him to see while blocking the entrance so he couldn't dart off. She began to scream at the top of her lungs, "I did not raise you to use drugs! All you're going to do is burn out and become nothing, absolutely nothing! Is that what you want? Is it?!"

Second to his dropping out of school, this discovery never left her lips and never made its way around the family circle. Shaking her head in disbelief, she would repeat with severity, "I know I raised you and your brothers better than that. I worked hard day and night to provide a place to live and food to put on our table and this is the way you thank me!"

This produced within him a feeling of total abandonment from a life once lived under a love that could never be lost. He thought that nothing in the world could make his mother turn her back on him and call him a good-for-nothing son. It was then he knew he had to get his drug situation under control before he distanced himself even further and lost complete control of his awareness.

Instead of getting better, however, his drug habit became a full- blown addiction. He started to act more of a fool than ever before. Not yet realizing the troubles that accompany slinging drugs and flashing money, all he chased after was a good time and a quick thrill.

He didn't have the slightest clue that society had its way of dealing with those who chose not to control themselves in a proper manner. Until that very first night, he always imagined that going to jail would solidify his name in the streets. After having been arrested several times, he now felt he knew exactly what not to do in that environment. Each time was nothing more than a misdemeanor charge except for one particular case that he'd never forget.

Upon hearing the jailor say there would be no bond until he appeared before the judge, he spent the remainder of the night restless and anxious. It was the longest night of his life. He trembled at the thought of being locked up and found himself in tears numerous times throughout the night. Not worried in the least about the money it would cost in the end, he had a much greater concern in mind. On this night, the reality of truth spoke to him directly.

Laying on a cot, eyes wide open, face drenched in tears and knowing that he was about to go to jail, he began speaking to God in a muffled voice in hopes that no one would hear him. Attempting to bargain with God, he carried on for five minutes or longer promising that if He let him out, he would begin to attend church…as if God had been begging him to go in the first place. He thought long and hard about how he would go back and tell his mother and grandmother they were right and that he was sorry for hurting them. Just like his mother had told him, he knew they'd raised him better than that. He then recited the Lord's Prayer, hoping that at any given moment he would hear, "Joshua Levi Benjamin, your bail has been posted."

After all, he realized, this was the real thing. "I'm in here," he thought, "and the drugs and money aren't doing me any good now." All he could think about as he heard keys rattling and doors slamming as the jailors made their rounds was this judge sitting up on his throne telling him what he could and could not do.

Then came the conviction of what he could have become if he had only listened to his mother's advice and finished school, joined the Armed Forces, gone off to college or even got married and started a family. She would often tell him, "It's a bad wind that never changes."

As he laid there crying and thinking about the predicament, he had gotten himself into, he could not come to grips with the situation and reason how he was going to get himself out of such a disaster. He wept, mourned, and worried in vain about what could not be rectified. In a desolate state of mind, he fell into a deep sleep where a dream began to shine through his never-ending thoughts. This dream presented a train of ideas, concepts and images, the likes of which he had never before seen or even imagined. It caused him to look at life from a different angle and through a different lens. Things that never mattered to him before now appeared in a new light.

With morning arriving later than ever, he awoke from a rough sleep to the sound of an abrupt opening of the metal cell door. The night had passed by calmly and it was once again time to face the new day. The sun was particularly bright on this day and shone through the jail windows with full intensity. Exiting his cell, Joshua began searching for the telephone area so he could make a call to his aunt who just so happened to live in the city where he was incarcerated.

He dialed the number pensively; fingers trembling with increasing intensity. The phone seemed to ring for a lifetime before she finally answered. She recognized his voice immediately. "Boy, what you doing calling me collect?" she demanded indignantly. With a rattling quiver in his voice, he replied softly, "I'm in jail downtown. I want you to call my mama. Tell her where I am and to come get me out of here, please."

His aunt, well aware of how he'd been living told him he ought to be ashamed. "Your mother is a hardworking woman and is trying to raise your brothers too," she said. "She don't have the money to be wasting on you just cause you out foolin' around, you know that! And, you know we were down at your mother's on Easter Sunday. She told me you're running around with this boy who just got out of jail. Is that what you want with your life, Joshua? If you carry on like this, you gonna end up in the same place as your friend."

Finally given a chance to speak after his aunt's colorful rant, he said with the quiver still strong in his speech, "No, no. This is not what I want… not at all what I want. "She responded, "I'll let your mother know you called and, where you called from. She ought to leave you in there…out there living like you don't know any better! Ever since your granddaddy died; you've gotten so much worse. He used to say you'd never amount to anything, that you're just sorry and you didn't want to work. I know she'll come and get you, but when she does, I want to have a word with you. You need someone that won't play around but tell you exactly how it is. You need to hear the truth, son." She paused for a moment before asking, "what are you in there for anyway?" "Drug possession," he replied. "DRUG POSSESSION?!," She screamed through the phone, "What are you doing out here with drugs? They don't play with drug dealers around here. They got all kinds of drug task forces up in here and each day somebody's dying over it. Drug dealers either kill one another or the police kill them. Even on my way home last Friday, I saw police running after some boys over on Campbellton Road."

He could tell his aunt was about to go on one of her famous critical rants and knew he had to interrupt her. This morning was not the time, "Auntie, Auntie...I know I've done wrong but could you please just call my mama for me?"

"Yes. I'll call her after while" she responded. "Give me a chance to get up, okay? You call me waking me up and I got to get ready for work... "But I will call her."

With that, he replied, "thank you very much. I love you Auntie!"
"Okay," she said. "Bye baby."
Getting off the phone, he glanced around the room inquisitively. Seeing no one he knew, he slowly made his way back to the cell in which he had spent what seemed to be an eternal night in deep thought. He sat on his bunk and began reflecting on the trials that lay ahead. Suddenly, he heard voices shouting vigorously from outside. "GET TO THE WALL!" The voice commanded. "EVERYBODY TO THE WALL...NOW! COME OUT OF YOUR CELLS AND STAND AT THE WALL, NOW!" Joshua asked the other detainee in his cell what was going on and learned that it was nothing but a typical shakedown, nothing out of the ordinary for this jail cell. They exited their cells in an orderly fashion to avoid rousing suspicion and in came

a police officer tossing over mats and blankets. After all the cells had been ransacked, the swarm of officers comprised of both men and women left the ward without a word.

As the detainees returned to their cells to fix up their bunks and put their things back in place, Joshua asked the others why this happened. His cellmate told him that during the night, with so many arrests being made, officers sometimes didn't get a chance to confiscate everything. "It's easy to miss stuff when you're bogged down," he said. This conversation turned out to be the beginning of a friendship that would keep him calm for the remainder of his detainment.

The two cellmates exchanged names, talked about how they had gotten arrested and discussed the severity of their charges. Before long, they had struck up a long, detailed dialogue about the drug game. They talked about how people loved getting high on cocaine cooked into rock. They agreed that drugs could make them riches beyond their imagination if only they sold them without getting caught. His new business associate reminded him, "the drug is produced to be sold, not smoked by the dealer."

This was sage advice every dealer would be wise to follow and Joshua agreed. They talked about getting connected with the infamous Miami Boys. This band of individuals arrived in town like a hurricane and Joshua Benjamin knew they were dangerous people. They set up shop in the projects and sold dope to everybody that passed by. The duo conversed throughout breakfast and lunch on a number of topics ranging from drugs to rap to girls and even family life. For the first time in his life, Joshua Benjamin was given the opportunity to get a feel of what people would say if they truly knew what he was holding inside.

2
Demand Awakened

Joshua's new friend went by the name of Justin Birdsong. As they continued talking and getting to know one another, they realized that perhaps, it's not all about dealing drugs and making money.

Family they discovered was the most important factor and this was something they could both discuss in great detail for a number of reasons. They both agreed that being broke and having next to nothing so early in life left little room for goals. The only goal they'd really reached was becoming adults and this stage of their lives was filled with grief and agony due to the decisions and choices they made in trying to live the thug life. Both were convinced that being goons would either get them killed or added to the rank and file of those who would spend their lives in and out of jail.

As the conversation grew deeper, Joshua tried ending it by saying he had to call his mother to see if she'd received his message so he could get out of there. "What about your girl?" Justin asked. He told him he didn't have a girl that would come get him out of jail and that all these girls he'd been messing with didn't have the strength or will to live the life he'd been living." They tell you they're down for whatever, you know? But when the money's gone, so are they." Joshua went on jokingly, "the honey starts running when the money gets funny."

He boasted to Justin about the first girl he had had a serious relationship with and how untrustworthy she turned out to be. He told him about the little boy that his most trusted family and friends claimed looked and acted just like him. They were clearly convinced that he was the boy's real daddy...and so was he.

The situation was too real for Joshua to deal with. Sometime after their break up, the girl had told Joshua that she believed he was the daddy but she simply loved another man. "Why didn't you have a blood test if you really think he might be yours?" Justin asked.

Justin, (Joshua started with a desolate expression on his face), I'm telling you, growing up without my father was bad enough and she told me they were getting married. I'd built my life on this false hope that the first girl I fell in love with would be the woman I would marry and keep for the rest of my life. This was not a love affair, but I loved the way this young woman made me feel. Understand I lacked no confidence in myself. From the summer of '84 she had me going crazy. I craved her sex more than anything. This sexy, young, brown goddess would give me my last taste of false hope." Joshua's walk down memory lane concluded when he told Justin that these girls would make you lose your mind if you are not careful. Walking away from the conversation toward the telephones, he jokingly said, "I think I'll give that nymphomaniac a call right now." He released an uncomfortable chuckle as he exited the room.

Holding the receiver in his right hand, he stated his name and waited to be connected. He knew that once his mother got started, all he could do was listen. Knowing she had already received the news of his arrest; he did what he could to mentally prepare himself ahead of time.

The first thing he heard when she picked up the phone was, "didn't I tell you about running around with that crowd? Joshua Benjamin, they told me you're being held without bond for drug possession and paraphernalia. I have told you over and over again to get a job and work, but I guess you have one now. Your aunt called this morning and told me you had to appear before the judge before you can be bailed out. The court clerk said it's a felony charge and that you're from another county."

With shame, Joshua replied, "I know I'm being held without bond until I go before the judge. They told me it might take three to four days. Will you please come and get me out of here? This is the worst place I've ever seen in my life. Please mama!"

She asked him where he'd been for the past two months. Before giving him a chance to answer, she launched into one of her all too familiar tongue lashings.

After listening to her yell, he almost wished that he had not even called her. Afterwards, she gave him a small hint of hope when she told him she'd consider getting him out. She was able to communicate with him again on a personal level after having heard many things about him from other family members. Wanting to ask him more about his involvement with drugs, she told him to call her back the following Monday. He didn't realize that his mother still wished to protect her baby boy from a vicious society. The last thing she wanted was to see his pitiful downfall.

After the call with his mother, he returned to his cell to sit and think about the charges pending against him. While sitting there in silence he thought about something his daddy had once told him: "There is no pie in the sky." This cliché never really meant anything to him until he sat pondering in that cell completely unaware of what was going to happen to him. He felt a profound void in his chest and he knew that only time could replenish it.

As he sat there thinking about his tomorrow and his past sorrows, he decided that, when he got out, he'd live just like his daddy did. Then, he abruptly realized he didn't, and possibly could never again trust a woman because of the pain and resentment his broken affair had caused him. "If I'm to get married and have children," he thought, "there must be a good woman somewhere out there for me." While spending the night mentally searching for the ideal characteristics of a wife, he pondered about what kind of man he was and how others perceived him. Included in these thoughts were the relationship he always wished he had had with his own father.

This arrest and the sobering thoughts had been long overdue. Up until this incident, he'd thought he could ride, get high and sell dope anywhere and everywhere. Little did he know the police here won't put up with dealers running the streets. If the officers that arrested him hadn't found the drugs and brought him in, this realization may have never taken place and caused him to wise up. He lay there sleeping off the exhausted expression clouding his mind until the morning sun rose over the hills.

3
A Mother's Love

Monday morning arrived. He heard a list of names being called and eagerly listened for his own while asking Justin what it was all about. Justin told him these were the people who would be going to see the judge to find out if they could post bail. Joshua was sure his name wouldn't be announced and quickly lost interest. He carried on with his business completely unaffected by what was going on in the background.

Finally, as if by accident, he heard his name announced loud and clear over the intercom: "Joshua Benjamin." With a cheesy grin on his face, he stepped forward as if he were already on his way home. At this point, any news was good news to him. He felt sure the judge would set the bond. While waiting to be transported to the courtroom, he asked the jailor how long it would take to get back to the jailhouse that afternoon.

"You'll be at the courthouse all day," he said. "They don't be in no hurry to put your black ass back on the street to do the same thing that got you in here. That's all you gonna do once they let your dumb ass out of here anyway." Rather than upsetting him with those undignified remarks, the words opened Joshua's eyes even further to the truth. To add to that, he came to the realization that this drug game was the real deal as he heard the judge declare that his bail was to be set at $105,500.

That evening Joshua, feeling great relief, was ecstatic to be going back to the jailhouse, strange as that may seem from a civilian's point-of-view. He started saying his goodbyes before talking to his mother about getting him out. Once he spoke with her and told her he had a bond set, he figured she could just come sign her name and get him right out. "It's that simple, right mama?" he asked. He didn't exactly understand how the justice system operated.

Being from another county made this trip to jail an eye-opening experience for him. He learned he could not change the rules and do as he please. He'd also learned that making money without knowledge was a quick way to get yourself into a world of trouble. He didn't understand the demands placed on the dealer and thought he could make enough to pay his way out of trouble whenever the need arose. He was in this cell and realized he did not know how or when he would be getting out. This terrified him on a genuine level. Hearing his mother tell him she could not sign the bond because she was from another county made him feel sheer desperation. He recalled feeling like he needed his daddy. He felt his father's assistance would be the only thing that could help get him out of this situation. After two collect calls from jail, somebody at home had taken the phone off the hook.

Knowing his mother was the one person who would never turn her back on him, he continued to call her asking her to see what she could do to help get him out. She informed him that she was only able to get a couple hundred dollars to assist in getting him out. He begged and pleaded with her to get the rest of the money to post his bail. Finally, that Friday, she told him she would get the money from her savings but insisted that he pay it back when he got out. He agreed and it only took one more day to get a bondsman to bail him out. At around 9 pm, that Saturday, Joshua heard something he'd longed to hear for the entire week. "Joshua Benjamin!" the voice boomed. "You have made bail.

Please come with me." He was then carried down to the booking area where he signed a few standard release papers before his departure. Seeing his mother and aunt brought him immediate joy followed by shame. He knew he had broken his mother's heart many times but this experience really taught him a lesson he would never forget.

"Nobody gives a damn about you like I do." Those were the first words his mother told him when he walked through the gates. Then, she quickly changed her expression and asked if he was hungry. She wanted to be sure her son was alright.

"I'm okay and I'm sorry," was the only thing he could say. As they rode out of the city, he had tears in his eyes as he looked at the image of hurt on his mother's face. Then and there, he vowed to never come back to the city for drugs or do anything illegal for as long as he lived. All he wanted at this point was to make everything better for his mother. And he knew his actions were causing her uncontrollable agony. Although he felt a great distance between them, she never left his side or let him down despite his numerous setbacks. He thought of something she'd told him many times before which brought a sobering reality to his distorted mind. She informed him that she was pregnant with him at the age of 19. No matter the potential hardships, she'd made up her mind to have the baby and nothing in the world could have stopped her. There were many times when things got way too overwhelming for her, but she always pushed through with that strong willpower she was known for.

Now, at the age of 20, Joshua wondered to himself: "What if she had given me up for adoption?" It was in this moment that he fully understood that there was nothing like a mother's love. With sorrow in his heart, he returned home with his mother in silence. Having brothers that looked up to him, he did not really know what to say to them at first and remained silent for a long time.

Instead of striking up a contrived conversation, Joshua went in to get cleaned up and ready for bed. For the next couple of weeks, he found himself running all over the place looking for a job. Feeling depressed and constantly out of the loop, he finally went to see one of his uncles who he knew had a steady job. After they talked for a while Joshua asked his uncle if he could help him get a job with the company he worked for. His uncle told him about the company and their policies.

"If you mean well and you're willing to do what's right," he said. "I'll help you get a good job. But Joshua, please don't let me down." His uncle was aware of how he had been living. Truthfully, Joshua had never tried to hide his involvement with drugs from his family. Still, he always made it a point to never bring drug-related activities around them in any way. Fools, his family was not! They knew there was no way for him to afford the type of lifestyle he was leading, having come from his background and no visible means of employment or inheritance.

4

Man Brings Forth a Child

With Joshua being release on bail, activities and conversations made a drastic change. He started to attend a local bible study and found a church to be a faithful servant. As he began to grow into a more responsible young man. Life's demands did not seem to be as stressful as before. The challenge of life had become Joshua new focus. He spent the next three to five years restoring his lost years of drugs selling and usage.

In the awakening of a new life experience of working a steady job and waiting for the paychecks. This gave Joshua to the reality of a much slower pace of life, but a more rewarding lifestyle. One that produced a wife and children along with the accomplishments of others friendly communication. The reward of home living was greater than the street life for him. He was also able to pay it forward in his social settings by becoming a volunteer and mentor.

Fast-forward to New Year's Eve in 1999. Joshua had just celebrated the most exciting day of his life with the birth of his son. Prior to receiving this child, which he was to raise and dedicate a central part of his life to, he was at a Bible study teaching the Holy Word to some men who were being rehabilitated.

The mission where the study was being held was one that Joshua loved to visit and support regularly. He and the mission's founder had similar passions and testimonies; both having been drug dealers turned users. The determination to go to war against drug usage and drug abuse had become Joshua's number one objective. He was full of zeal and hope for anyone that hinted they had a drug issue. With hope and wishing, he believed he could help everyone with this dreadful problem.

The passion and drive to help their brothers, who had lost their place in society, was rooted deeply in both of their lives. It went all the way back to the men who were instrumental in their respective childhoods.

His grandfather, who was the epitome of fatherhood for young Joshua, taught him the importance of reading the Bible daily, living a life that demanded respect, providing for his family and having a single wife and a set of children which he loved dearly. Joshua often recalled one of the most memorable lessons he'd received from his grandfather.

A girl from Joshua's school, who was the daughter of one of his uncle's friends, had visited their home one day. Being a shy boy at the time, Joshua ran and hid under the house. When the girl and her family had left, he returned to play with his brother and cousin. While they were playing basketball, the boys were making fun of him for apparently having a crush on the girl. After playing basketball for a while, they all sat around with their grandfather who proceeded to tell them that Joshua did the right thing by running and hiding. His grandfather added that the day was coming when he would not run from the emotion but allow the emotion to run him to girls. Joshua did not understand what his grandfather was trying to convey given that he was only 11 or 12 at the time. His grandfather was full of wisdom and old family folk tales that he loved to share.

Joshua loved his grandfather dearly but could not put up with his style of discipline. He would whip you with anything. One time, he even whipped Joshua with a stalk of bell peppers. Once, Joshua was trying to stop a fight between his brother and one of his cousins. As he was trying to separate them, his grandfather approached. He didn't ask any questions. He just reached down, pulled up a stalk of peppers he had prepared ahead of time, and said, "I brought y'all out here to work." His brother and cousin ran; they knew too well he would go off. Joshua stood there, dumb founded, trying to explain the situation thoroughly so that there would be no doubts of what was really going on, but his grandfather wasn't having it and just started whipping him frantically. As he struck him, peppers went flying everywhere.

Joshua learned a valuable lesson that day. When they got home and finished up their chores, they all ate supper together and had a discussion over the table. While listening to his grandfather talk about life and how the fields were looking, he became angrier and angrier. To make matters worse, his brother made the mistake of asking why he'd whipped Joshua. "He was not doing what I told him to do," his grandfather said. "I told him to chop grass away from the pepper plants. All he had to do was cut the grass. Let them fight if they want. I told them to do the same damn thing. But when I started whipping him, they went right back to work, you see?" Their grandfather told them that the whipping helped all three of them, be it directly or indirectly. This incident taught Joshua to do what he was asked by his superiors and, more profoundly, to stay focused on his goals. Farm work was something his grandfather took very seriously, and Joshua didn't understand this sort of impassioned dedication until he was older and wiser.

Furthermore, his grandfather never had a significant amount of land to work with and explained to Joshua that in life you take what you have and you turn it into what you want it to be. Starting out with little more than a single acre of land, his determination to be successful at his trade drove him to find plots all over town to rent and farm. As he observed his grandfather's efforts to take care of his wife and grandchildren, Joshua found himself proud to have his grandfather's name. He was often heard saying his name loudly and walking with his bony chest stuck out in showing pride that he was a Benjamin. His grandmother, on the other hand, was his love.

She would always talk about their family and how they were going to stay together forever in this harmonious environment that was the family farm. True love was her song to the whole family. One day she heard him proudly exclaim that he was a Benjamin. She stopped to explain to him that, although he was part of the Benjamin bloodline, his daddy was a Bellamy and not a Benjamin.

"Well yeah, I know my daddy's name," he reasoned. "But I have my granddaddy's name." Still, she went on to tell him that he was really a Bellamy by blood and tried assuring him that his father's name was also commendable as he too was a hardworking family man. This statement made him say something he had never said before while conversing with his grandmother.

"If he was a good man," Joshua asked, "why did he father me by another woman?" His voice displayed little emotion. She started off by letting him know she was going to tell him something he wouldn't understand until he was older. "People sometimes do things they later regret," she answered. "It's not easy to explain, my dear boy. Still, young Joshua had too many questions and, unfortunately, his grandmother didn't have all the answers.

She suddenly changed the conversation by asking Joshua a question of her own. She knew he saw married men and women sneaking around with other people. "Will you promise me that when you are old enough to marry, you will not do the same thing you see these men and women doing out here?" she asked. "It's terribly wrong." "Yes ma'am," he assured her. "When I'm older and I get married, I want my children to have my name and the same mother. All of them." She told him that a good name is earned and not always handed down.

"You could start your own name," she suggested with great emotion. "Even though you are a Bellamy, you're still a first-generation Benjamin so, technically speaking, you could start your own family tree." By saying this, Joshua's grandmother was conveying to him that he could do something better than his father. He became more inquisitive about the bloodline upon hearing his grandmother telling him he could be the first. With this new found knowledge of who Joshua Levi Benjamin really was came a series of serious examinations into his life. No longer would he feel down when people called him out or shouted to him that he was nothing but a black bastard. Following her conversation, he fell into deep thought concerning the subjects of family and fatherhood. Her words would remain with him for weeks to come.

"They'll never be able to make the same statement against my children," he whispered to himself. He continued thinking about the actions of the men he saw in his life.

Eventually, his aunt's husband and his brother took him to work with them. The place where they were employed had a special place during summer months where young men could come for work. Not only did they help him with summer employment, but they would often take him fishing and keep check on how he was doing in school. Joshua recalled getting into a fight. He knew he had to beat the boy or he would never live it down. Coincidentally, the boy did not show up to school the next day. His uncle's brother was waiting outside after school to hear about the fight, but Joshua broke the news that the boy wasn't there. "You better be ready when you see him again," he warned.

Not wanting to let him down, Joshua went to the football game that Friday night with scrapping and brawling on his mind. When Joshua saw the kid talking with a few other guys, he approached them and shoved the boy that had beaten him up.

"What's up now?" he said with red in his eyes. The fight was on. They threw a couple of punches back and forth and eventually locked up. The others had pulled them apart and one of the boys that separated them said, "Y'all will end up going to jail for fighting out here." But Joshua knew this was more than a fight. He knew that his manhood was being tested. He had been taught that you never allow anyone to put fear in your heart. That fight served as a catalyst in Joshua's life, leading to him being known as someone who handled his business. While working his summer job, he worked with some older guys that liked to drink. During one of their outings, one of the guys got drunk and began to talk tough until he lost a patch of hair from his head. When he got to work the next morning, he told Joshua how he had been in a fight the night before. Joshua asked the man, "What happened?" But he didn't particularly want to talk about the fight. He just lifted his hair in the back and revealed a bald spot.

When Joshua saw the red spot, he asked the man, "So what are you going to do about your hair being pulled out?" He told Joshua he didn't know the man's name and Joshua started to laugh, and he just kept laughing to himself for a while, reflecting back on how he had been taught to deal with such situations in the past. He stopped and got serious though when he saw the hurt on the man's face. Joshua then looked the man straight in the eyes and said sternly, "you don't have to know his name. Tonight, just don't drink. And as soon as you see the man, who did that to you, go up to him and punch him in the mouth. Do it as hard as you can. Don't think about it...just do it! That red spot don't look too good. One thing I've learned is that, if you let people treat you how ever they want, they will take advantage of you without a second thought. But I mean, he can't be that bad of a man. After all, he just pulled your hair out, it's not like he knocked out a tooth or anything."

Joshua had gained the respect of these older guys when he had to put aside his hardball method of handling unfavorable situations. He, his brother and a young Mexican were working together on an assignment from one of their higher-ups. Joshua looked out for the two of them and refused to let anybody put them down. He also looked out for them financially. Anytime he got work for himself, he would let them in to split the earnings for the job.

One day, the man they were working for told a friend of his he had two niggers and a wetback working for him. Joshua thought about hitting the man in the face with the broom he was using to sweep the deck, but instead he approached the man and said, "you know, you don't have to speak against us in a derogatory manner." The others knew he was hurt because his brother and the young Mexican looked up to him and they knew what his emotions were like. But they admired the way he used his words to intelligently defend them without raising an angry hand.

5
City Life Spoiling

With Joshua maturing and becoming more responsible, his mother allowed him and his brother to live with their aunt in the city for the summer that followed. They were allowed to go there to find some work. This first time away from home had exposed him to both a world and an environment, which he grew to love and long for. He was able to travel each day by bus and train, meeting and speaking with all kinds of different people as he made his transitions through life. The ones he loved to listen to the most were the street evangelists and hustlers from the projects.

At times, he would get off the bus at the train station and watch the minister's debate while preaching the word of God with such vigor that he would lose track of time and have to catch a later train. As he spoke candidly with the people, he was meeting, he would listen to and try to understand each of their viewpoints with an open mind. He had watched people argue and fight his entire life, but seeing the brothers standing out there with the Bible in hand proving their point shed new light for Joshua to use whenever he disagreed with someone. From watching street evangelists, he learned that if you really know what you're talking about then you wouldn't have to raise your voice. This learning experience would serve as a platform for him as he continued to grow and learn.

While watching the street evangelists, Joshua would be so infatuated with what they were saying that he would go out and repeat what he'd heard to other people. Though he was delighted by it to a great degree, it turned out that such controversial oratory was not as evoking as the stories and lies spread by the hustlers. They not only enlightened him, but also took him in as a young blood, showed him love and gave him some action. With Joshua being from the country and new to city life, they loved to answer his questions. During that time, he was selling produce to earn money which sufficed for him until he decided he wanted to fit in a little more. It took all the money he earned at work just to look and dress like those gangsters he looked up to.

As he continued his weekly tenure with them, their relationship grew to become like that of a university professor and an undergraduate student. They were his mentors and he was their apprentice. Not to mention, whenever they needed something handled, they trusted Joshua to do it. By the time Joshua turned 20, the only thing that really mattered to him was getting all the money he could. He had no real plans, no goals to look forward to in life; just putting in work and doing dirt. He informed his friends back home of the money to be made from hustling drugs. Soon, he was setting up deals which landed him a hefty profit. With $28,000 in his pocket and a plane ticket to Springfield, Massachusetts, Joshua knew he had to sober up quick or he just might lose everything he had worked so long for.

During this trip, he'd learn a few things – chief among them was the fact that at that moment, his life didn't matter to anyone else out there in them streets.

The money, action, and drama Joshua had seen back home paled in comparison to that of organized gangsters in the greater metropolitan areas. The work he saw up in Boston left him with the desire to be nothing less than a straight up gangster. Joshua had gotten a long- distance call from a person in Boston. Some connection in the north had gone bad and his presence was required there. At first, he was baffled when the man on the phone called him Big Country. Joshua knew he had to pay close attention to what was being said. Only illegal people called him out! That title was earned for doing one specific job very well.

He learned right away how serious that the situations had become. His business ventures went so well that he flew back to the Hartsfield airport and purchased another round-trip ticket. This time, he went on vacation to sunny Orlando, Florida, where he had the most adventurous time staying at the Howard Johnson Hotel. This hotel absolutely blew his mind. A young fool in a city where no one knew him meant he could do anything and be anyone without any consequence.

Having never gone on a vacation before and not knowing what to do with himself, he just hung around the hotel for the first couple days. While touring

the pools and the Jacuzzi on the third day, a younger man in the hot water, partying with three pretty girls invited him in. Joshua reluctantly and very slowly stepped into the warm water with them. At the same time, he had thought
of a statement his grandmother once made about young, fast girls. She told him some girls have this certain curiosity within them which causes them to jump from one man to the other.

Once he was in with them and the conversing took way, Joshua moved into a new world; a different sort of realm. He stepped into a place where the prettier the girls were, the more distanced he felt from reality. He knew about his grandfather, his uncles and a few other individuals he respected greatly, who had gone and had sex with the same easy women many times over. He knew he did not want to get caught up in the same sexual desires.

He asked them their names and then told them his own. As the conversation progressed, he asked them where they were from. "New York City," said one of the girls…then all three of them broke into a dance and began to chant something he couldn't quite make out at the time. All he could really do to avoid appearing uncomfortable was stare at the water glistening and rolling off their bodies. The girls then sat back down in the Jacuzzi and giggled. Joshua then turned and asked the guy in the Jacuzzi where he was from. He said he was from Dallas, Texas but it was clear Joshua was more interested in getting closer with these girls than chatting.

He told them excitedly that he was on vacation and planned on going to Disney World there. They replied saying that they had already visited some theme parks while they were in town.

Joshua sighed and asked what their plans were for the next two days. He believed this conversation was a golden opportunity to use the game he'd learned from watching the street hustlers.

He spent the rest of the evening trying to captivate them with his keen sense of humor by using his snappiest southern colloquialisms in hopes of competing with the hustlers. If he could pull it off and have sex with one of these girls, then his triumph would quickly be made known when he got back. But since none of the three girls was giving him the slightest hint of interest that they were physically attracted, he changed the conversation with haste and exited the pool area as quickly as possible without turning back for a split second.

The next day, the fellow from Texas informed him that he liked the way he was talking to the girls the night before. He told Joshua that, if the girls didn't have a chaperon, "we could be with them." "Man, why didn't you tell me this yesterday?!" Joshua was infuriated. "The girls in that Jacuzzi opened so many doors for you last night." Joshua looked at the younger man attentively, whom he addressed as Texas. "Do you want to be with one of them New York girls?" he asked. A big smile covered his innocent face as he bobbed his head and started to blush. With just a hint of shame, Joshua asked if the girls had said anything about him after he'd left. "They talked about you all night," Texas quickly blurted out. "They were also asking about you this morning and wondering where you were." He went on to inform Joshua that they would be back at the pool by 6 o'clock that evening.

"We can be there too, if you would like," Joshua added. Texas appreciated both, the way Joshua talked to the girls, and about the girls. He wore an even bigger grin on his face than before as he bobbed his head steadily as if he was feeling the beat of the music bumping in the background.

"Texas," Joshua addressed his new friend in a warm tone, "those girls are in for some moaning and groaning tonight." He laughed obnoxiously with his new friend. For the rest of the afternoon, they sat around and discussed being on vacation to pass the time until the magical moment when they could return to their beauties in the Jacuzzi. Not wanting to negatively influence another brother's life, Joshua abruptly got serious about what was about to happen. He asked Texas about his parents…most of all about his relationship with his father.

Joshua went on to tell him that he grew up without his father's involvement and learned how to survive from some of the most down to earth men that ever lived. He then started to reminisce about how he had learned first-hand how to woo a young woman. Joshua boldly told him that the girls wanted to be with us just as much as we wanted to be with them. His statement carried an air of extreme confidence.

"Man, you have to create an atmosphere the girl will want to be in and then lure her in with your charm," he assured Texas. "Paint a picture with your words that will never leave her mind. She will go anywhere you lead her, and it will forever be the place she wants to be."

Joshua found himself telling the younger man what the older people in his life had taught him. He now felt like he was in their position and had the moral obligation to pass on this wisdom to his peers. He even told him to protect himself from diseases and unworthy females while he was out and about.

As the two spoke, Joshua shared some of his personal experiences. He told him the story of a time when he was hanging out with one of his cousins and how, at the time, they thought they had a chance to have sex with this girl. But she rejected them immediately after they exposed their intent. With his cousin being very sexually active and already having fathered two children at such an unbearably young age, Joshua kicked back and followed his lead. He said to his friend that no man trained him in this area of life. "I learned how to deal and communicate with girls as I watched one of the greatest paymasters."

Joshua told him that his cousin was known to toss out money and follow up to convince and overtake these gullible females. The conversation took a rapid turn when he advised his friend to take care of himself and not be led astray by powerful sexual desires. His eyes showed a sincere generosity and he let out an airy sigh as he bowed his head pensively.

6

A Fatherless Son Reunited

Joshua returned home content from his first and only vacation. Back on the street and armed with the mentality to be more than a simple errand boy, he saw hustling in the streets as vain and failing in comparison to the organized racketeering with which he'd interacted in Boston. This trip up north was what Joshua later recalled as his first true eye-opener into the drug game. Seeking to be more organized in his illegal activities, Joshua found himself in contact with a deputy and a police officer. As he worked on building his own organized front to protect him from the judicial system, he began buying his drugs from the policeman and his associates.

As these relationships grew, there came a day when Joshua took the initiative and robbed somebody. Once the county sheriff's department received news that Joshua was involved in the robbery, he was immediately brought in for questioning. Consequently, the officer who was dispatched to pick up Joshua was also his business partner. When they arrived at the jail, he was carried to a back room, interrogated and let go without any issue. The officer had done all this instead of delivering him directly to the jailor to be arraigned and have his fingerprints taken. Not only did he let him go, but he personally took him back home in the squad car. Two or three weeks later, Joshua and the officer met in a bordering town to set up another deal.

Out of all the different men in his life, giving him varying degrees of influence, the one with the greatest impact was undoubtedly his father. Not knowing his father until he was a teenager brought closure to the thoughts, ideas and concepts that had been festering in his mind since infancy.

The life changing experience of meeting his father and being a part of his life made him finally feel wanted in this world. As their relationship continued to improve, Joshua watched his father very closely and his father did the same to him. Joshua greatly respected his father for having received him into his life at this point. Unaware of which conversation had transpired to bring them together, he knew this was a serious time in his life, though he'd always had his mother's protection from the very start.

One day, she sat him down at the dinner table and made known to him that his daddy was coming to pick him up for the weekend. Joshua was shocked and could not help but wonder what exactly brought about this change in his mother.

Though he was now united with his father, he still couldn't help but feel that something was missing – especially after having grown up without him. This abiding void, combined with the pressure of being a teenager without a mother chaperoning his weekends, fueled his endeavors indefinitely. But he now had a sense of what it was like to have such a man; such a father figure in his life. He was thinking like Tony

Montana…the world was his and he could conquer the unconquerable. He knew there was a life out there waiting to be lived and that society would cater to his every desire, so long as he could pay the bill.

This new sense of being accepted by someone who had always been seen from a distance empowered his youthful imagination and opened him to valuable new concepts and ideas.

PART II

7
Life Demands Initiation

The young, black man's initiation into society is of utmost importance. We are faced with the reconstruction of a savage generation and its offspring becoming increasingly more bent on self-destruction. We are forced from within our broken humanity to seek solutions as desperate men of this day and age. The financial state of today's youth is of negligible importance to them.

As we deepen our awareness of the state of being of a man who is to become a leader, we observe that he is not your everyday, "run-of- the-mill" youngster. Oppression, depression and suppression consistently plague him. Many of these men are full of fears, animosity and low self-esteem. All of these elements constitute the wealth of emotions balled up inside today's youth.

The social order of today is in such disarray that these young men are powerless and insensitive to the real dilemmas of society. With guns and bullets so easily accessible, the concept of life and death bear minimal meaning to a generation of rogues and savages.

The sorrow we are witnessing, and experiencing is the direct result of the family structure's collapse. The family power structure is being cocooned in this cold, dim capsule of violence and survives with little to no accountability. Once the metamorphosis has taken place, the child is often left to caterpillar his way through life's growth processes. It is simply miraculous that God's plan of procreation is one order which cannot be altered by man.

Now, speaking as a man having gone through the caterpillar stage and advancing to the experience of the butterfly on two different spectrums in a single lifetime, I can assure the certainty of this claim. The first spectrum: being born to a single mother and the father of another wonderful family; a family to which I have been warmly welcomed and have loved beyond measure since the age of 13. The second spectrum: A result of the predisposition of my family structure. When a young man is presented to the forefront of society, a society where survival of the fittest is the only real way of life, and where there is no father in place to give initiation to the life of the young man, that baby boy lacks and longs for something that is critical to the success of his maturation. Being completely unaware, this young man's pattern in life is being drawn out one line at a time.

The reformation of the knowledge of how to transcend the generation gap of fathers initiating their sons currently finds itself in dire straits. We are not the first generation, which God calls unto man, a broken father-son society. Frederick Augustus Washington Bailey is the birth name of a man who most inspired me to be my son's father. He coined the phrase, "It's easier to build strong children than to repair broken men," Frederick Douglass is the name most people knew him by."

The immense tragedy in the life of a son raised up in a society without his father's initiation is never recognized early enough. Many times, he receives said initiation from other men prevalent in his life to help him man up and understand his responsibilities. With foreign impartation and intense emotions reveling up inside him, he is affected drastically by the absence of his father's presence balancing out his character. This leaves him to grow up with a mentally unceasing war inside that would never have existed had he been reared with a true father-son relationship. "I am the product of an environment filled with all kinds of characters," he'll think to himself.

Once a young boy is given the opportunity to see how other males are living and handling all types of daily situations, he is provided with other options to guide and protect him.

All men are conceived and brought forth into life in the same manner as the rest. Initially, he appears as an embryo with the cover and protection of a loving mother. He is clearly more than a mere thought as she has the honor and privilege of announcing him to the world on the birthday of this gift from God. Secondly, the child goes through a rapid growth period which is the most impressionable time of his entire life. Now, he is interacting with a society that will permanently shape his personality, his attitude, his emotions and his character in general.

Discipline and guidance at this time in one's life is essential to overall well-being and will follow them for the rest of their lives for they are the prime elements which set boundaries. Furthermore, it is critical that boundaries and respect are properly established at an early age. When boundaries are justly established, the child will come to understand that fire is hot after the first time he touches it. He will have been shown by example that it is important to stay away from those things which cause pain or risk paying the price. Receiving these instructions and adjustments from one's father is among life's greatest privileges. But not having the option to choose to be in the presence of one's father is pure tragedy. This is why the son will forever long and pray for his father's approval.

With essential boundaries being set into place during the man's youth, he soon wanders into the educational stage. At this point, his behavior will determine the strengthening or weakening of his character. I can recall being a young school boy. It was without a doubt, the best time of my life. I went off to school to learn and play. Then I came home to learn and play some more. I just wanted to learn all I could. With the sheer excitement of gaining knowledge, I learned to read extensively. In fact, my love of reading was one of the reasons why I was able to escape a lot of the negative aspects of life.

Consequently, there was also a lot of stuff I was not exposed to growing up. Still, I was somewhat a rebellious teenager and many of the areas, in which boundaries were not set early on, quickly became accessible and more desirable to me. This led to problems. During a certain point in the growth process, you are almost exclusively the product of your environment.

Looking back at the development of my life, I see with transparent clarity the effect of not being fully raised by my biological father. I was the one who received life's trials from other men – some family and some friends of family. Then I had to make some serious life-altering decisions. Without the knowledge of how my father subdued and conquered his fears and turmoil, I was left with the unique experience of being reared by a strong and dedicated single mother. She is something like Jabez's mother, that's with her heart and soul constantly filled with tears and fears of how and what to do for her son. According to my own recollection, her love and desire for me was the key factor in the success of my childhood.

I know I will always occupy a special place in her heart that nobody can ever replace. Knowing and feeling that pure expression of love is sometimes the only thing a young man in society has that he can trust with undeniable certainty. This loving impartation received from her care and discipline has been, and continues to be, the sole factor which empowers me when I find myself wrapped up in deep, emotional despair.

Manhood, on the other hand, is the time when you are to act as shelter for others. This proves arduous when your own journey into adulthood was fueled with anger, hurt and a deep animosity that you don't exactly comprehend.

8

A Loveless Generation

Many of today's young adults grow up feeling that society owes them something or that they deserve things they have never worked to obtain. They were raised with a sense of entitlement and once they enter adulthood, they are left on their own even though many of them still live with their mothers or grandmothers. In the worst cases, some of these millennials are left to their own devices just wandering the streets from place to place and couch to couch. This is a terrible situation and it is further compounded by their natural, lustful desires and the consequences that accompany these most crucial decisions.

As we know, the pride of life will always find its way to attract others to us. With these attractions comes the knowledge of how to communicate with people, and as we further our advances, the attraction increases simultaneously. When two people enjoy their connection with one another, it illustrates the radiance of love to all who witness it. Love has a beauty of its own and can make others aware of its manifestation between two lovers.

Unfortunately, many find themselves absent from the true essence of love. Even when the spreading of love has not made up an integral part of a young man's life, there continues to remain the God- given touch of love and life from the mother. The great tragedy of contemporary romance especially for the youth finds its expression in the difficulty of sharing something they have yet to receive. The emptiness syndrome, as well as the distractions associated with fear, tension, anxiety and distress are constantly embroiled and tugging on the demands of man. In fact, all societies are suffering from their fears.

Love has not altered its purpose or meaning with the changing of the times. It still has the same effect on people who are willing to permit the time and space for such amorous and caring involvement. The lifestyles we choose now determine to what degree of love we are willing to express and share with others.

I am reminded of a young man I have read about in several books. He was put in charge of a leadership position by his mentor. This young man had been trained in faith by his mother and grandmother, and the faith that had been shared with him fueled his subsequent success. The reception of love that is offered is exceedingly important for all human beings. The youth of today are being educated on how to have success and even the cruelest of teachers shar love when explaining to someone the correct way of doing something. This goes to show that love finds its proper expression in more than one form. It should be stressed to all that 'empty lives' are never without hope.

There is a Heavenly Father who sits high and looks low. He observes our situations so fervently that we can feel Him before He makes His presence explicitly known. He patiently awaits our despairing cries so he can proceed to bring us forth to salvation. God has a need for all young men, both broken and whole; whose circumstances and personal predispositions often rest beyond their control and lead them to feel intimidated. Many also experience a potent combination of pain and sorrow during these times of intimidation with reality. Having these battles going on in our heads and in our hearts leaves us feeling uncared for and without the comfort of love. This form of isolation drowns young men in anxiety and overwhelms them with fear (F.E.A.R.): that is, "False. Evidence. Appearing. Real." Perfect love casts out fear. But we know that fear has its own outstanding torments.

9

The Emptiness Syndrome

The so-called "super-highway" of social media, in addition to the pressing demands of life, bombard us on a daily basis with merchandise straight out of our wildest desires; some to purchase and others solely to dream about. As we pursue a life of health, wealth and happiness, we are frequently greeted by numerous forms of media. They are packed with unique opportunities – some good and some not so good. Once you have picked out what you want and added it to your cart, you may come to find that your hopes have been let down. These products often leave us feeling quite empty, especially once the originality of it has passed and it no longer carries that special demeanor it once had.

In today's world of social media, it is not as important, as I have observed, to be first. I have seen a person become depressed because their Instagram, their Kick, their Twitter or their Facebook post was not liked or shared as much as they would have preferred. This is a prime example of social media locking you in a false love based on receiving a certain number of likes or followers or reposts on your page. Some people get a small taste of fame in this way, and to watch it decline is the most distressing position of all for them. Sometimes their sensual desires and focus of being liked on social media give them a false sense of connection, both with society and with reality. The love of oneself is the most important like you will ever receive. When you relinquish your focus of likes and reposts, the rollercoaster of emotions starts to scream with an air of enthusiasm. The social coastal ride will end. However, when it ends, many will walk away thrilled discussing how delightful and fun it was. Other want to get right back on for another jaw-dropping experience, but there is a long line to return. Today's society can give you the sense of immediate stardom.

Once enticement is conceived, the ideas come flowing in. The chain of thoughts crammed in the procession of the why and how brings to mind the means of how to accomplish everything. With these ideas and dreams subjectively pressing on many young, impressionable minds, eerie feelings find their way in.

A society that is perpetuating and displaying lifestyles of success, oftentimes without merit, is enough to draw anyone a clear passage to being overtaken with error. Life is so delicate, and nowadays we handle it without thinking of the end game of each situation. Some of the events that left us broken would not have caused sorrow if we had thought a little more about them at the time of their occurrence. Then, we could respond with a clearer perception of what the result would most likely be. For instance, we could do with a little more conversation and patience.

Coming to grips with the real reason we are only able to talk after 7 p.m. will help keep our conscience clear of guilt. Entreating others with dignity, before getting together, is the best way of detouring empty feelings such as those we are forced to move on from after a love affair has come to its bitter conclusion. Regardless, by being ignorant, we invite and endure the sorrows associated with our desires to indulge in our lustful fantasies. Without taking the time to think, we prefer to act on impulse and do whatever comes to mind at a moment's notice. We are then carried off to a sobering reflection following the event, especially when something negative occurs as the result. That's not to say that everything we do in the moment is bad and will leave us feeling empty, but rather that we will undoubtedly come to think of it later and this may carry certain consequences with it.

One thing in life that has the capacity to isolate us in our thoughts, even after it is long gone, is love. You know yourself, that the emotional rollercoaster has come to the end of the road and nothing in the world can fill that void. I am not talking about just good sex. While it is admittedly a vital part of a lasting relationship, you can buy wonderful sex. I am referring to times when feelings are at an all-time low, a time when there is no song, poem or person that has the power to overcome your void. No drink, drug, social setting or form of media has enough toxin to make you forget. Then, that special moment happens: the one you love says, "We're going to make it. I have your heart to care for. I love you!" Then comes all the small talk we so frequently take for granted and, before we know it, the thrill is over and everything falls apart, shattering violently as it hits the floor one last time.

When the feeling of not being loved by another overwhelms you and engulfs your life in shriveling darkness, it takes a supernatural and divine encounter to empower you and bring you back to waking reality. You find the same love that tore you apart so miserably in the past washing away before the tide of love and care shown by others.

A song comes to mind as I continue to collect my scattered thoughts: "It Don't Hurt Now," by Teddy Pendergrass. With eyes full of tears and a burdening weight beyond measure in my heart, I remember a love that lost. It explains how such an unrecoverable love can lead to sleepless nights and days without meals.

As we course our way through life, there are challenges we are forced to face every day. These challenges cause us to make critical decisions, the results of which always have the potential to follow us for the rest of our lives. Sometimes we make the wise choice; other times we make the wrong choice. The wise choice keeps us afloat, while the wrong choice makes us sink. Most wish not to bring up their wrong choices given that the typical outcome is frustrating, disappointing and shameful. The pain and lasting memories of negative choices showed me that sharing my mistakes can help others discover alternative paths and deter them from making the same choices.

"Flocks and herds were the foundation of the Jews' prosperity". So, throughout the Old Testament, we are presented with a clear portrait of what a good shepherd is and how one behaves. For example, good shepherds watch their flock at night. They chase away predators. They gather the weak ones in their arms and they go looking for that which is lost." (Jones, 183) God disapproves of those shepherds who stuff themselves and care nothing for their herds. In our society, it is so easy to get caught up in counting sheep that we tend to lose sight of their condition. I know of pastors who are more centered on bringing more members into the church rather than saving people. Many have forgotten the true meaning of being a shepherd as being one who takes care of the flock; a servant and a watchman.

"Thus, says the Lord God: 'Behold, I am against the shepherds and I will require My flock at their hand; I will cause them to cease feeding the sheep, and the shepherds shall feed themselves no more; for I will deliver My flock from their mouths, that they may no longer be food for them." (Ezekiel 34:10, NKJV).

God is not against shepherds having grand houses, nice cars, and fancy clothes. He wants things to be in line with His will in terms of leading and caring for the sheep. God wants us to be faithful in all that He has given us.

In life, we will make mistakes, and nothing can change that. But it is important that we acknowledge them, correct them and most importantly that we learn from them. We are not perfect, but God gives us the wisdom to take care of ourselves and our responsibilities.

10
Live Your Life

One breezy Saturday morning, I was sitting in a chair at the barber's shop waiting to get a haircut. A client entered aggressively and began speaking with an extreme air of profanity. The barber, pointing in my direction, told him I was a minister. The young man came over to where I was sitting and said something, I'd heard many times before. I've heard it from guys cursing on the job, at sporting events and even just sitting around chatting. However, this young man's demeanor touched me in a different way when he muttered softly, with his eyes directed at mine, "forgive me, please."

The sudden humbling change in his countenance was so profound that I responded to him with a statement that caused a righteous uproar in the shop. I simply said to him, "live your life. "This is a major theme of mine. I wanted to comfort the young man so as to ward off that awful feeling of embarrassment and shame one feels after such a chance occurrence. Without the minimal knowledge of who I was or what I did, he began stuttering to me that he didn't mean any disrespect and he was sorry. As I sat listening to him, the Holy Spirit convicted me at once. I sat there in a pensive state wondering what I could say to this young man during this favorable window of opportunity.

As my son sat in the barber chair next to me, he was also tuned in to the conversation. With my intense desire for community and unity among us, I proceeded to fervently discuss character and the power of its preeminence.

First impressions are always important. In today's society, we forfeit many opportunities to help and empower our fellow man. In order for me to display characteristics of the man our society demands; I must already have accepted God and His power. Without an endowment from Him, we would all remain powerless and utterly hopeless.

As my son and I drove away from the barber shop, he began speaking to me about the change he observed. When we began this dialogue, it was already clear to me this was a high point in my life. Him being a deep thinker, I knew beforehand his questioning would demand substance. His educational goals always pushed him to seek wisdom and strive for a positive character. Needless to say, "live your life" is something he hears often from me.

Our conversation didn't stop at the man in the barber shop not having initial control over his character. When confronted with moments like these where I see an exploitable opportunity, I take full advantage. Not only am I trying to be the man my society demands, but I have the honor and privilege of helping my son become the man his peers and his own generation will certainly demand.

Being 33 years older doesn't give me an endless wealth of knowledge in today's society to be handling such instruction, but I can't just walk away and expect him to grow and thrive with the same opportunities as the rest. I'm living life with my wife, my daughters and my sons at the forefront of my heart. My age simply endows me with the wisdom to let it all out in the presence of my children, especially my son during such trying times of his young life.

During the indefinite hours of our talks, we would share moments of both triumph and failure. Riding around town and taking road trips together are our most enlightening times. Not only do I get to indulge in the joys of being there to laugh and joke with him, I also have the opportunity to share my weaknesses. It is both painful for me and a mere joy to reveal to him my biggest areas of failure. In the end, the joy of sharing life experiences with him gives me relief and reminds me how important it is to guide him.

As a teenager, I endured all that life demanded of me without the teachings of a father. I was reared in the home of a very powerful single, black mother. She reared five children altogether. Though we were poor, I am blessed to say we were not in poverty. She taught me the importance of being educated and her favorite line to me, "live and let live," helped me survive some dangerous situations during my upbringing. Her wit, intuition and desire for me to become a successful young man gave me the sensitivity to do the right thing in most cases. But, like most young men, peer pressure entangled me in its web of regret. Now I am faced with the golden opportunity of being a father who has the capacity to guide and support his children.

11
Societal Suicide by Reason

It was all accurately accounted for and adding up to a successful summer: the summer of '88 in full view. Everything was lining up just right; driver's license received, a nice young lady found, and I was making some good money. With this sort of mindset, and my heart fixed on indulging in the high life, I wasn't expecting such a grave reality check.

The news that day was given to me in the most abrupt way I couldn't have possibly imagined. I got a call from one of my cousins informing me that another one of our cousins L.B. had committed suicide the night before. With this shameful update, my world was turned upside down. My ecstatic train of thoughts were completely derailed. I truly admired L.B. He was four years older than me and always had to take the spotlight and be the life of every party. I loved explaining his name to people who wouldn't believe that L. B. Johnson was his real name.

The family gathering for the funeral and the preparations prior were almost unbearable for such a young dreamer to witness. Sitting around in disbelief over what had happened, I just remained in silence and listened to the older gentlemen converse with one another as they spoke and shared stories of seeing the younger generations coming up and thriving. The remainder of the following evenings were spent at our grandparent's home.

These were quite possibly the longest weeks of my life, and very soon came the moment of facing the questions and answers behind everything that had occurred. We knew this moment was coming, and finally on the third day following L.B.'s suicide, my great uncle gave way to the dialogue:

"All of you guys come out to the talking bench," and he walked out without another word. Sitting on the bench outside, my brothers and several of our cousins began to sob involuntarily. Being summoned to the bench is, and always has been something of a sacred moment, as well as being a natural place of solidarity. Every time you're asked to meet there, you know to prepare for resolution. This time, they approached the conversation with ears only because this was one of those situations they never could have imagined. Consequently, they didn't have the words. To be sitting out there with everybody discussing our cousin taking his own life was a surreal moment. Many of us simply couldn't get out thoughts together. All of us sitting and standing around the bench did our best to hold back our emotions and listened attentively. This was serious and we knew it.

Our uncle began with a solemn address: "Man up." With tears of sorrow on our downcast faces, we all looked directly at him when he uttered these two powerful words. In his deep, military-charged voice, he declared that he understood the pain and disappointment that everybody was going through.

"But young men," he started. "Listen to what I'm about to tell you and take it to heart. Now, with what you all have before you, all I ask of the rest of you is to stay awake! In these desolating days, the evil games being played will take you in and play you until you either give up or give out."

His speech had begun and it was clear he had a lot more to say." Because of the delicate and lavish lifestyle, you young fools chose to adapt to, in many instances, you will be used like someone's favorite towel. I'm not gonna go and point you in any direction because I know I'll just get mad and cuss you all out. Your older cousin's death doesn't have to be a constant reminder of how fragile life is. You all know good and well how young and tough L. B. Johnson was out here in these streets every day. Let this tragedy serve as a warning to you. Believe me, I am as hurt and probably grieving deeper than any of you boys. But, after all is said and done, you have a life of your own to live and enjoy."

As we began to trace our steps back toward the house to rejoin family and friends, we tipped the red cups in our hands back to pour a libation to our fallen street general. We could not hold ourselves back from going into a laughing fit as we reminisced on behalf of L.B. Johnson. He had a mean streak that we as comrades knew not to cross or push too far. But that's not to say he would have fought one of us for having spoken about the characteristic flaws of his lifestyle.

The respect we surrender unto one another keeps us from certain topics and conversations of that manner. Most of us, brothers and cousins alike, had grown up in separate homes from our fathers, and this was just another common factor in which we all shared.

Days after the funeral and sudden family reunion, we decided to call a meeting to talk about the suicide together. This was not a call to party, nor was it a time of gathering to boast about our lives and talk about what was new. We all met up at a park at a reasonable time so that our cousins, who had real jobs, could make it out as well. Many of us, however, chose not to earn our way through society, and therefore tended to have more flexible schedules. The same thing that happened to our cousin could happen to any one of us. We were all aware of that!

Our meeting started with a question from a 12-year-old boy. He chimed in by asking profoundly, "If a person is always happy and has pretty girls around, why would he kill himself?" One of our older cousins told the young boy to hold that thought for a moment. He went on to say that happiness is a state of being that we want to stay in forever.

But life has its fair share of situations with a large part of them being pressing. He was looking deeply into his younger cousin's eyes and noticed how he began to rapidly tear up. There is a powerful force held by that emotional fluid. With slurred speech, he gave the boy an eye-opening lesson. He said, "You like that young lady I be seeing you walking around the park with?" A big smile suddenly appeared on both of their faces simultaneously. "That's joy," he went on. "Joy is better than happiness. It's something deep down inside of you that must be cherished at every opportunity.

Now, to the rest of you love birds, we didn't come out to play the birds and the bees. While the stage is set, I'll write a play across your young innocent minds. I know that some of you have a so-called girlfriend. These young, beautiful, sexy independent females will help you lose yourself every single time you decide to lose focus. It's not that it's a bad thing, trust me. All I'm saying is there is nothing wrong with carrying on, just don't get carried away.

Yes sir, young men will be young men and carry themselves with pride and honor. I will not sit here and tell you all that L. B. Johnson was a perfect brother, cousin or friend. He had his days when it seemed nothing was in his favor. From losing jobs and relationships to resorting to selling drugs, his life was in a constant limbo. All that changed after one visit from a group of unorganized robbers that approached one of your uncle's drug houses. Seeing how critical it was to stay in control and handle yourself in the drug game in the face of all dangers that come with it, L. B. told us all, and I quote, "Y'all must be crazy living like this...no rules, no talking it out, nothing."

L. B. learned in the 1980's that, if you wanted to be the alpha male of the pack, the cost would be completely changing your character. He was not ready to become a drug dealer. And he wasn't really set out for it from the start. He was a Johnson, true to the family name and claim.

When L.B. realized in the society of the 80's that, if you wanted to become the alpha male of the pack, you would have to become a completely different person, he realized he was not cut out for this lifestyle; or, at least, he was not yet ready for it. Though he was true to his name, nobody preceding him in the Johnson family ever resorted to ending their own life, no matter the distance they felt from reality. With the gathering of young men becoming more emotional, I asked everybody within our circle of influence; brothers and cousins, fathers and uncles, if anyone had issues or problems overwhelming them. If there was ever a time to speak out, it was then. The tranquility became serious in an instant. I looked at each of their faces and, at that moment, I felt a desire within myself to cry, to just wail out. Not only because of the loss of our cousin, but simply seeing how much these young black men were suffering and absorbing so much in that moment made me feel a sort of resolve. My thoughts absorbing all the positive energy around me, my anxiety of crying in front of them vanished instantly. Before I could say anything concerning the pressures, I felt in my own life, the tear drops slowly began descending from the corners of my eyes. I was usually too bashful to cry in front of others, but sometimes you just have to bite the bullet.

With everybody staring into my eyes, the only thing I could utter was, "your life is too important." I shielded my face with both hands, hoping to wipe away the tears with the abrupt movement of my hands. The emotional waterfall had crested, the sponge of my intellect was at full capacity. They seemed in complete awe to hear and see us so mentally broken, yet without shame. It was absolutely gratifying. With people watching you, it is near impossible to hide the flaws. But I have some valuable lessons that have slowly been attained through life and to share these lessons with others is the only way to spread the wisdom. The greatest lesson, however, has been to just be real to myself.

12

If a Man Loves a Woman

As a little boy of about 10-years-old, I observed one of my uncles endure the pain of losing the love of his life. He later shared this experience with me during a conversation in which he was discussing marital life with me and giving me some valuable advice. He told me that, if I loved my wife with all my heart and wealth and spent quality time assuring her of that love, we would have a wonderful and prosperous life together. Before it was time for me to have a wife, the love of my life, I endured countless relationships that made me think infinitely and ultimately feel invincibly numb to the sensation while others left me feeling low. "I had to look up the see the bottom."

There were moments of my life, some intentional and many unintentional, which made me wonder endlessly. Nevertheless, I didn't exactly receive proper instruction in this area of my life. I've suffered severely due to the lack of knowledge in dealing with the amorous relationship scenario.

As a teenager I was exposed to a number of positive male role models. Many young men of my day would love to have had the same privilege. The ideas and mannerisms I learned from them were not so positive, however. Some of them were dogmatic in their actions in dealing with ladies and the ones with the nonchalant attitudes and subtle approaches always held my attention the most. The charm that I constantly observed in my presence was simply inevitable and I had to practice and formulate my own soft side in order to woo the young ladies. At this point, all I wanted was to give and take the love.

Communication and emotions grow and we soon come to find there are two words beginning with the letter 'L' that bring people together. One holds the divine power to keep it together permanently and permits the passing of time to make it stronger. The other has an unimaginable passion and a certain self-inclination that merely feeds itself until the lasciviousness departs or the object of one's desires changes. Consequently, this is typically the cause of its own demise. These two words are love and lust.

When two people are attracted to one another, that alone is a wonderful feeling to share in. Your stomach turns over, your head is held euphorically in the air, and there is a sincere sense that this is all we wish to live for. The impassioned exchange of words is ever so charming and, in these moments, the love and the lust forms an unbreakable bond between the two. Others look on with amazement at the infatuation of the newly formed relationship. The two tend to become overwhelmed with the passion of this sensual, and soon to be sexual, explosion. Now that the chasing has begun, there is a novel sense of being the man this relationship demands. All I await is consummation with the hope that this will go on forever. As this hope escalates exponentially and the feeling of trust between the two prevails, manhood develops and unfolds naturally. This is precisely what occurred with my female counterpart, causing her to melt from within and entrust me with a piece of her heart as I continued adding fuel to the incessant fire.

Within my brain raged a typhoon and my thoughts became stirred up severely, firing up every motion and desire in my bones. With pride in my chest, lust in my eyes, and control of my own flesh, my sole determination was to bring my sex life back into forward motion. She was on fire too. She was being spoiled with attention and accolades. We shared the same cares in this relationship and an intoxicating sort of solacement burned within her and brought me higher than I ever could have imagined. One evening, as she embraced me with care and compassion, the touch overwhelmed us both and we commenced making love.

For days, weeks, and before we knew it, months, we found ourselves delving deeper into this heated sexual escapade. Nothing less than love and happiness was our song. As the passing of the day followed the descent of night, our lives continued to follow their course. On every occasion we took full advantage of the moment with one heart, one mind, and one love. Before long, lovemaking had grossly overtaken us.

For about six months it was love and happiness, sunshine and rainbows. For the six months that followed it was more like, "how can you mend a broken heart? "Once the way we made love changed, I realized we were growing apart. Questioning the love that seemed so everlasting left me hopeless and consistently checking my heart for faults. Then came the emptiness, that shrouded void which knows no limits and no way out of the distressed mind. Constant rejection and ignorance on the part of the past lover gives way and opens a void that cannot be locked and shut.

As time passed and anxiety attacks ran violent in my head, music became my main source of comfort and acted as my sole escape from a harsh world. While listening to Keith Sweat one solemn night, the track "How Deep Is Your Love" came on shuffle and spoke to me clearly in words I had been meaning to say for such a long time but could never articulate when need be. It went like this:

Been all day thinkin', all night wonderin', Why love has to change.
You kiss me but it's not real, Tell me what happened.
Are we living a lie, baby?
Is that magic gone?
Oh, do you feel the same way you used to, girl? Oh, tell me, is it wrong for us to love like this?
How deep is your love (How deep is your love)?
How deep is your love (How deep is your love)?

How deep is your love (How deep is your love)?
Oh... oh... oh... oh... (How deep is your love)?

The pains which encompass a young man's heart sometimes leaves him feeling destitute and in complete solitude. As the hours turned to days and the days turned to weeks, months rapidly began to fly by, and human nature reminded me more and more of my desire to love and to be loved. My confidence in being the object of a young woman's desires gave way to a grand awakening.

One early morning, at the crack of dawn, I heard a motivational speaker on television say, "live your dream." Being freshly out of a failed relationship and finally over the shock of potentially living a life of desolate loneliness, I once again began having dreams of living with a wife and having beautiful children of my own. With undying hopes tied to this dream, my quest regarding its realization soon began yet again. As I began to socialize more and force myself into the nightlife and the party scene, I came across the same egocentric and self-destructive lifestyles that led to such pain and misery in my past and the past of so many others. These outings began clashing with my dreams, leaving me in something of a dilemma where I knew what it was, I wanted, but was not in the place to receive it. I fretted through life with the hope of being kept ashore by the constant image of couples and lovers enjoying one another's company. I knew that that could be me and my determination to live the life I desired reignited.

Living and loving the nightlife brings thrills and spills at every turn. The standard of this lifestyle enlarged my array, and to receive any truth from the extremities of life portrayed in the streets, you would have to be a magician. The ostentations which display the highest level of splendor smeared my conscience and gifted me the privilege of hoping and believing that, out of clubbing and boisterous young women, a flawless wife would somehow emerge.

Finally, without any effort on my part, this fine young lady sat next to me one night, a night which was most certainly planned by someone with a certain intent in her mind. "Hello!" she shouted to me in a flamboyant tone. All I could do was give her a gesture so as to say something along the lines of, "What's up?" I knew that if I opened my mouth, nothing would come out. As she and her friends carried on and embraced the night together, I could not stop my mind from running circles in my head. The thoughts were racing in and out, and though I tried to come up with something to say as they began their steady walk back toward the table, nothing came out once again.

A few minutes later, our eyes met and we stared into each other's eyes. Finally, almost by chance, our dreams of enjoying having someone by our side with care in their heart met and began holding hands. It was a very strange coincidence how this simultaneous chemical reaction took place within both of us, but the magnetic field of attraction brought us together at the right time. Suddenly, I felt a discomforting desire to turn and run from this opportunity forever, but I held my ground and fought against this feeling, though it felt like a tide crashing in on my heart. Every atom of my being scorned me, pessimistically declaring that this would go no further.

Now that we had been watching one another for several hours, we made the move almost at the same exact time to connect and engage in a conversation which seemed to have no ending as the drinks kept pouring in.

This was no ordinary club that offered hookups or potential connections for promiscuous late-night meetings. It seemed to hold something more within its mystical walls. We agreed to exchange numbers and set something up in the near future. After this meeting, I immediately went back to living the fast life.

I'd occasionally think about that night, but not enough to give her a call just yet. The pain stemming from my last rejection continuously flared up and led to a sort of dismal procrastination and the denial of happiness by means of a visit to her place, or anywhere in public for that matter. It's a strange thing how the power of thoughts work.

While sitting down in my living room a couple of weeks later, some of my favorite blues classics began to play. Muddy Waters' song "19 Years Old" came on I found myself dashing over to the cassette player to hit the fast-forward button and skip the song. This frivolous action happened for two reasons. My first love was 19 years old, and this new girl was also 19.

As I released the button and walked away, "Long Distant Call" started playing. Though I felt a strong desire to fast-forward again and go directly to the next track, I decided to sit down and listen to the words, carefully observing the powerful delivery of this blues giant. I was used to hearing this song; the older guys would play blues all the time when I was growing up and even still to this day. "Now," I thought, laughing and jamming by myself, "it's my turn to blues and booze."

Not just to mimic these older cats with their tall hats shaking sorrowfully in tune with their heads, but at the time I was feeling dejected to the point of being unable to make a call to Ms. Waters, the beautiful young lady I'd been waiting to get the nerve to contact after that magical night in the club.

As the music played in the background, I picked up the receiver from the phone attached to the wall and, dialing the number and hearing the ringer bounce back and forth slowly, an intense nervous shutter ran through my bones and anxiety set in at once. On the last ring I considered hanging up the phone, but I held on for a split second longer and heard a male voice on the other end of the line sounding like Mr. Barry White.

"Hello?" he said inquisitively.

"What in the world?" I thought to myself.

"Hello, hello. Anybody there?" he repeated.

"Hi," I muttered nervously. "May I speak with Renee, please?

I heard him call out to her and, just before handing her the phone, he whispered. "some peanut wants to talk to you. Don't be on the phone long." It had been two months since she last heard my voice, but when she answered she immediately said in a natural tone, as if she had been expecting my call all day, "Hello, Joshua." I was so astonished that she had announced my name that I nearly lost my wits. With that salutation came a strong feeling of encouragement, stability, and, most of all, self-worth. With a feeling like Superman, having the power to conquer any obstacle life put before me, I winded up just standing there listening to her without making so much as a mutter.

"Why did it take so long for you to call?" she asked me. "I've been waiting so long," she emphasized.

I felt the excitement of our connection sparking back up as I held the receiver to my ear and heard her sweet, delicate voice speaking to me in a familiar tone. With calm and patience in my voice, I kindly asked if we could meet and have a chat. She accepted without the slightest hint of hesitation. As it happens naturally when love firstly arrives to the heart of a man, I immediately began to plan for our meeting.

Our outings became more frequent and increasingly more desirable with our conversations growing deeper and more varied. We would find ourselves talking about the future, such as our dreams and where we see ourselves in the next couple of years. I was a twenty-two- year-old hustler and she was a beautiful nineteen-year-old sophomore at a historically black college. We were clearly very incompatible, though we tried to hide it. She had hopes of becoming an optometrist; I had hopes of being like Al Capone, with whom I share a birthday. After carefully considering that all I had to offer was years of tears and fears, I spent an entire sleepless night thinking long and hard about our next date. Regardless, we started going out more.

One night, while dining at a family restaurant in a small adjacent town, I exposed to her a grotesque, realistic picture of my life. I couldn't help but feel she had to be aware of this before we let anything major transpire between the two of us.

"I know you and your brother," she interrupted me quickly. Apparently, she had caught wind of us operating in the hustling game sometime in the past and she went on to tell me things even I had no knowledge about. For example, she recounted to me how another hustler from my hometown had attended the same black college as her and she knew as much as anyone about me being high and selling drugs in the projects. I was trying my best to keep her out of everything I was involved in at the time, which had the potential to cause real problems for her. On the other hand, she was trying to become a serious part of my life, complete with all the danger and drama that go with it. As we wrapped up our discussion, I knew without fail that I would go no further with this relationship. I was nobody's fool and I was not about to be hustled for someone else's success. This was how I felt and I remained adamant about it.

My longing to find my life partner was postponed until the winter of 1990; February 15, 1990, to be exact. On that gorgeous evening, with the sun high in the sky and a bitter chill in the air, a dear sister of mine picked me up for Bible study. Before heading over to the church, she had to make a stop at her mother-in-law's house. She asked me to get out with her for a few minutes, so I did. Upon exiting the car, I noticed these girls looking out a window in my direction. Once inside, I sat in the drawing room of the large house as my sister, accompanied by her mother-in-law, continued through a separate door. I waited patiently, tapping my feet and bobbing my head in silence, as she visited them in another part of the house.

After about twenty minutes, she finally returned to where I had been sitting with a group of girls accompanying her. She told them I was her brother and that I would be going to Bible study with them. Then she introduced me, and as we proceeded to leave, I could hear them giggling and talking distinctly. I was genuinely shocked as they were members of the same church, and this was my first encounter of the sort, though not my last.

Following Bible study, we had another opportunity to chat. As we talked, I discovered their ages, and these age differences hastily threw up a barrier which I respected. However, I did take notice of, and to this day cannot forget, the striking beauty of one of them. This was what I consider my third divine encounter with God. He had saved my soul two months earlier and I knew, in fact, I had told myself on several occasions that I was not going to miss out on these golden opportunities anymore. I needed to take what life threw at me in a practical manner, and not for granted.

After understanding that God had made a young woman so astonishingly beautiful, I prayed that He make me responsible for her so as to bless me with a gorgeous wife. For the three years that followed, I studied the Bible intensively. I prayed, I fasted, and I no longer had to fight against loneliness. God had somehow constructed a love for his word within my spirit and, with that love, I wanted nothing more than to live with a family of my own under His authority.

One evening, during the spring of 1992, I visited the same house of my sister's mother-in-law. During this visit, I got the chance to speak with her brother-in-law, who was my mentor at the time. After speaking with him and leaving for work, I went through the dining room where I saw LaToya sitting down doing homework. We engaged in a casual conversation, but it soon transpired into something beyond anything I'd ever felt before.

As we talked and exchanged thoughts, she told me she was getting ready to go to prom. I asked if she was going with a boyfriend and she told me she wasn't. The conversation carried on and my time ran short; I knew I had to leave for work sooner than later. I felt myself getting closer to her somehow and, after another moment of talking, I stood up in haste and, to my surprise, she stood up as well. I started walking by her to head out the door and I got the sudden urge to turn around and hug her, so I did. It was the most magnificent hug of my life and to this day I can't truly explain what made it so special at the time. I held on for about ten seconds. To me, it was more than a hug. In that hug were entangled my hopes, my dreams, and my love. As I held her tightly, I whispered in her ear, "I like you." Then, something within finally allowed me to let go

.

That afternoon changed my world forever. I no longer felt the chilling cruelty of rejection. This young lady made me feel that my love had finally come out from the deepest reaches of my being. With that intense feeling in mind, as well as her aspiring youth, I tried hard not to interfere with her dreams and, specifically, her education. With God's guidance and a great thirst or righteousness, we found ourselves capable of avoiding getting involved too soon.

Next came the roughest patch of my love for her. She graduated and went off to college. Surprisingly, another young man came between us and my world once again appeared to have taken a pitiful turn for sadness. Regardless, that thirst for righteousness sustained me without fail. It kept me studying God's word fervently and living in His world while external fears and doubt tried without fail to deter me.

The real enemy, the devil, always comes prepared with his wiles. Again, he taunts me, and again the word of God comforts me and keeps me focused on the right path. While my love was put on the backburner, God closed out another disaster in my life. Although He saved me from street life, he still had to sever the streets from me. God used these trying times to empower my being, both mentally and physically, and deliver me for good. I learned to pray better and entrust God with everything.

One of the many scriptures that opened my eyes and helped push me through these trying times was as follows: "Likewise the Spirit also helpeth our infirmities: for we know not what we should pray for as we ought: but the Spirit itself maketh intercession for us with groanings which cannot be uttered."

13

When Stake is Higher than Demand

Being a young black man in a world tugging for power on all sides can and will leave one powerless in the incessant battle for life. Life should never leave you feeling decimated. Unfortunately, there are times when others make decisions that affect what you have at stake. The most important people in my life are my wife and my children, the little ones who didn't choose me but love me regardless. At times, they think profoundly and come to the reality that God chose me as their father. My role in our essential existence is keeping with the structure and culture given to us.

Watching our children grow has been one of my greatest joys and most devoted prayers. Now in their teenage years, they ask me to teach them things they have not yet learned or experienced and this often leaves me feeling genuinely powerless. Then, that light ignites and I realize I do know what to tell them because I have taught them the value of truth, that is, the value of knowing what is right and holding on to it no matter what. Despite what may oppose you on your path, do not break, for the truth is worth holding on to.

I've suffered losses and major setbacks in life that I continue to share openly with my family. Through every trial, tribulation, failure, and defeat, we have yet to let go of God's immortal hand. The divine interventions and continued grace of God has led us to triumph and permitted us to overcome all the trials of our common enemy. Everything has not always worked out in our favor, however. Even after losing jobs, cars, and being put out on the streets, we have held on to our dignity and, consequently, have not lost our sanity.

I have traversed through life at a steady pace and there has always been two spectrums of man which have never failed to bring to my mind a certain conviction. Both spectrums have made me wiser as I experience and observe life respiring around me. The first spectrum is the rich man who lost his focus on what's at stake over what's in demand. Then there is the poor man, to whom fate has landed a position in life with many more opportunities to come. The demand on his life is to persevere in order to take care of all he has at stake, that being the mere existence of his life. I observe both states of being with scrutiny, particularly when tragedy overwhelms me.

The poor man's state of happiness depends on his primitive survival. On the other end of the spectrum is a man whose happiness depends on the materialistic survival of his things. Some days, the poor man's resolve is, "if only I could get a meal. Just something to fill the void in my stomach." The rich man's greatest appetite, however, is not aimed at the consumption of food; he has plenty to waste. This appetite is rather his steady accumulation of riches, and when his quest for wealth becomes hindered, his joys become sorrows.

Now, a very careful study of the Bible provides me with the following advice to further analyze this scenario: "For wisdom is a defense, and money is a defense: but the "Excellency" of knowledge is that wisdom giveth life to them that have it."

14
Aftermath of a Drug War

The high life comes at a price. If you're not careful, you'll spend a lifetime paying for it. And when you are careful, you'll spend a lifetime in warfare. Being delivered from the drug culture will empower and guide you through the torn lives of others. Reflecting on it, it's clear that the hallucinogenic wave of the 80's drug culture gave birth to a generation of young thugs our society wasn't ready to deal with. Being high on cocaine and flashing money was all a young fool wanted to do.

On the 1st of April in the year 1984, I had two painful experiences. First, I received some bad news over the radio. The announcer stated that a famous musical giant was killed. I later learned that the use of drugs may have motivated the tragedy. Second, I got my first taste of the cocaine culture during my teenage years. These two events occurred at such an impressionable age and caused another killer to emerge from a life fixated on poverty and low self-esteem.

Growing up in my grandfather's house, I learned first-hand to take what you have and make what you please. He read the Bible at a scholarly level and discussed the scripture with everyone who would converse about it. This was especially shocking because he struggled to read anything else, not to mention he couldn't even write his own name legibly. But in our small community, he was honored as a man who had his house and his family in order. To the surprise of most, he was also a bootlegger.

The actions observed in my early childhood served as a catalyst to my later lifestyle and desire to earn money and hold power. My grandfather would sit in his chair in the evenings and read the Bible. Sometimes he would call for me and tell me to go get a chair. As I returned with the chair, the whole family would be present and sit around attentively. With us all in place, we would listen and take in the wisdom and instruction he preached, and he would go on to tell us about current news and explain what he expected from us.

As I transitioned from adolescence to being a young adult, I saw my grandfather endure a level of animosity that ruined the lives of some of the older gangsters of his time. In the spring, I turned 15. He suffered some kind of physical illness and later died of a heart attack. He left us before I had the chance to show off my "gangsterism" and all the money I expected to be making. I found myself seeking social acceptance and wishing to grow up being respected. Therefore, I was forced to celebrate with the hustlers and gangsters who knew him so well. He never disrespected others, nor was he ever dissed by anyone.

Then, at 16, I'd find myself sitting around listening to millionaires telling their recycled stories of how they came up. After running some small errands for them and always being right back in place for the next task, I was finally asked to go drive one of the club owner's cars. As we drove to the city to pick up a new car, they began speaking about my family's involvement in an event that should have made us millionaires, but my grandfather was ultimately ousted. That conversation ignited a burning desire within me to redeem my grandfather's name and restore his glory.

On the way back, I was driving in the Lincoln Continental Mark VII following the club owner and his friends in their new Lincoln Town Car. As I was driving, I remember thinking to myself what a privilege it was to know these men. They made several stops in other towns on the way back, but I was really just enjoying myself and the luxury of the vehicle. They were wearing high-class suits and hats with long feathers on the side. Mr. P would ask me every time they made a stop, "Are you doing okay?" "Yes sir, Mr. P. I'm doing just fine," I would respond each time. He would always remark how much I reminded him of my grandfather.

In the last town before we got home, we made one last stop. He told me to wait at the restaurant right where I was. Thirty minutes had passed and they finally returned to the restaurant with two cars following them. They parked and Mr. P. waved for me to come over. He introduced us all and pointed me out in particular to a man that went by the denomination of Little Benjamin.

He told the group that followed how he had been taking care of me and it turned out they already knew me because they had worked with my grandfather in the past as well.

It didn't take long to realize that this was no ordinary introduction, but that it was an initiation. The other two men weren't new to me either. I'd never spoke with them, but they knew my family well and had seen me and my grandfather together.

By the time the exchange had ended, Mr. P. was happier than I had ever seen him. I couldn't help but wonder what it was all about as I continued driving back to the club. Upon arrival they exited their Lincoln with an air of dignity, still laughing and reminiscing about the old days, and Mr. P. came over to the passenger side of the car I was driving, got in, and put a stack of money in my hand. He told me to take this car to his house and then come straight back to the club. As he walked away, I pulled the money from my pocket and, to my great surprise, I found five $100 bills. I quickly put it into my pocket, leaving my hand in with the money to make sure it didn't fall out.

Upon returning to the club, I noticed that the smiling faces had become serious again; this was the norm with this crowd. This was the first time I had heard outside of my own family, "What you see here stays here." The events that happened next never left my mind. The actions that transpired before me awoke a warrior within that society wasn't yet prepared for. A deep connection sparked and, before I knew it, I was placed in a leadership position with the power and authority to make critical decisions. This magnitude of authority being passed on to a young fool will almost always lead to hurt and suffering, but little did I know that this was not some spin-the-wheel game of chance.

At this level, you are chosen. I didn't understand at the time that there was a malicious sort of ranking system in which I had involved myself. While sitting with some peers one day, laughing and joking around, a young brother got offended and pulled out his gun shouting ferociously, "call me weak now! Call me weak now!" It was the worst mistake of his life, and his last, as well as the hardest day of our teenage years. The funeral wasn't long after and a trial soon followed.

The loss of life became a regular occurrence for many teens and young adults, in particular the males in our community. With death rates spiking all around, we sought safety and a more secure territory. Once our new-haven was determined and confirmed to be a good place for business, the trap was set in more ways than we ever imagined.

Our activities were being observed by some very powerful hitters in the drug game with a greater supply source than we had. We were approached one Thursday evening about some business that was to be carried out for them. They told us about some people who had gone missing and asked menacingly if we wanted to be next. These were more organized dealers than we were and, by the looks of it, they were definitely killers. Them becoming our new suppliers put us in another league and we were prospering beyond our imagination, though we constantly had to be vigilant and watch each other's backs.

With the flow of traffic increasing all the time, the flow of gangbangers and petty thieves saw an increase too. At this time, our plans were to make enough money to get out of the game and stop hustling. Our plan would have worked out fine if these suppliers hadn't been greedy and gotten themselves more involved than we initially had planned. They continued bringing more drugs and, as a necessary consequence, more protection. Finally, just as these suppliers had suddenly come into our lives without invitation, they exited just as quickly and without a farewell, providing us a convenient way out. These guys had the best protection available and the highest quality of resources which, without warning, destroyed them in an instant.

The unspoken code of the streets in the 80's was more honorable than today. Not to mislead you or make you feel that hustling drugs was a good start to life in my teenage years; rather, it was set to fail from the start for me. I went to jail three times between the ages of 18 and 20. Between the ages of 21 and 23, I went another four times, these times being much more incriminating than the last. My last time being arrested for drugs was in the fall of 89, the same year George H. W. Bush was elected our 41st President. This last time in jail, I was no longer concerned with getting out. I was arrested for drug possession and, at that point, I was using more than I was selling.

With a look of aggravation, they replied, "get back over there and go to sleep. Don't nobody here know you like that, "I was so certain that my name was called. I got up and went to the showers to clean myself up. I then sat down on the mat to think about what was going on with my life.

That afternoon, the heavens opened up for me, a good-for-nothing user. A minister visiting the detainees came prepared with Bibles and spoke to us about Jesus and God's plan for salvation. He gave us the chance to ask questions and I asked him with great curiosity if it really worked.

"It has worked for me for years, and without fail!" he answered with great enthusiasm.

"May I ask you one more question?" I asked timidly. "Will God save and forgive me too?"

With the same enthusiasm in his voice, he exclaimed, "of course, my son. He will forgive you and he will save your soul." Then, after assuring me of

God's plan for salvation, he orated the sinner's prayer with me: "That if thou shalt confess with thy mouth the Lord Jesus, and shalt believe in thine heart that God hath raised him from the dead, thou shalt be saved. For with the heart man believeth unto righteousness; and with the mouth confession is made unto salvation. For the scripture saith, whosoever believeth in him shall not be ashamed. For whosoever shall call upon the name of the Lord shall be saved."

15

The Demand on My Life

As the year 2014 reached its final days, I anticipated a wonderful and spectacular celebration with my son. This was his 16th birthday and we had talked briefly in the past about getting him his first car. Unfortunately, this saw a delay due to some job-related issues. I'm aware his hopes and expectations were somewhat deferred, but one thing I've always done with him was be real and straightforward. I always let him know where I was, in both good and bad times. He knew I had been harassed and unjustly fired. He made me proud on several occasions and I always made sure he knew that without the slightest doubt. I tell him I'm proud of him and that I love him all the time.

We discussed the state of our financial affairs and prayed for the positive economic recovery of our family. He understands that money is a cruel master when it is the controlling factor and he also knows that it is a wonderful servant when handled properly. He has an idea about setting and reaching goals and, whenever he desires something costly, he thinks it through thoroughly before inquiring. Once his plan is set, he will sometimes tell me, and at other times he will just ask for the card to order something online, but he always has a definite purpose in mind that he follows through with passionately.

My girls have also continued to bless my soul and make me a prouder father every day. Their compassion and understanding of life and the importance of setting goals has enabled them to excel beyond my initial expectations. As I converse with them, I listen with great attention and increasingly realize how difficult it is to be an adolescent in today's society. I see clearly that both peer pressure and pure pressure in today's youth is much more complicated than it was in my day.

While rearing our children, my wife and I would stop in a moment's notice when one of them needed our attention. We would assist them to our best capacity and then return to whatever we were doing prior. As they continued to grow, the same trend seemed to follow. We always taught them the importance of family and unity and stressed that we could accomplish more as a unit than as an individual.

In today's society, we are demanded to adapt to a fast-paced lifestyle and change our ways in order to maintain the standard of a God-selected family. I often text and call them at random times, usually for no concrete reason besides keeping our connection intact and deeply rooted with the passing of each blessed day. With social media access constantly in our hands, it is much easier to deliver a caring message to them, not to mention quick as lightning.

However, we are not only called on and chosen by God to raise our children. God has also chosen us to be a vital part of building a 1st-century church in a 21st-century world. Along with four other families, God allowed us to found and establish a church in the month of March 2002. It has been a wonderful journey thus far. The church has won over many optimistic souls and equipped them to serve the Lord.

Over the past 13 years, God has promoted me from minister to the office of apostle and district overseer. The commissioning and elevation came as the result of my seeking God's will for a greater revelation of Him and seeking to educate the next generation of leaders. Not only has God used me as a church leader, He has allowed me to raise up other leaders who have gone out into society to raise disciples for God.

The anointing is a direct response of reading and studying God's word with passion and fervor. "How shall a young man cleanse his way? By taking heed and keeping watch [on himself] according to your word [conforming his life to it]."

"Study and be eager and do your utmost to present yourself to God approved (tested by trial), a workman who has no cause to be ashamed, correctly, analyzing, and accurately dividing [rightly handling and skillfully teaching] the Word of Truth."

"We are assured and know that [God being a partner in their labor] all things work together and are [fitting into a plan] for good to and for those who love God and are called according to [His] design and purpose.

For those whom He foreknew [of whom He was aware and loved beforehand], He also destined from the beginning [foreordaining them] to be molded into the image of His Son [and share inwardly His likeness], that He might become the firstborn among many brethren. And those whom He thus foreordained, He also called; and those whom He called, He also justified (acquitted, made righteous, putting them into right standing with Himself). And those whom He justified, He also glorified [raising them to a heavenly dignity and condition or state of being]."

The transition from youth minister to Pastor happened as the result of establishing a Bible study in the Blalock's home in Greenville, GA. The study quickly became a church by the end of the first year. Subsequently, we had to find a building in which to hold a worship service.

It turned out to be more difficult than I'd imagined. Nevertheless, everything in the Blalock's home was going great and the Bible study was attracting positive faces. I didn't think twice when the conversation about starting a worship service was initially presented. One of the open visions God had given me earlier in my salvation journey was that I would someday establish a church in His name. As we continued to pray about finding a suitable building, the local City Hall moved into a vacated school building containing a cafeteria which they would rent out to various organizations. This was a positive break for our organization and helped us fulfill our social purpose.

Faced with an overwhelming promotion, I asked my original Pastor, Apostle Leonard, to consecrate me in the office of Pastor. He not only consecrated me, but he sat me down and asked me about my journey and my confidence in leading a church. He went on to teach me in more profound detail of the importance of living a life worthy of God's presence. With that admonition in mind for the several years that followed, God allowed me to meet a host of Pastors and leaders.

During a conference in Savannah, Georgia, as I was receiving word from one of God's mighty women, I was directed to step up in a chair. As I rose steadily, she spoke to me in a gentle voice saying that the way I had physically elevated myself was a just reflection of God's plan to carry me to the next stage of my righteous and holy journey. Within two months, I was invited to attend my first ACTS Network Leadership Summit. At around lunchtime, I asked the wonderfully-mannered lady next to me if I could buy her lunch. She accepted without hesitation and, during our lunch, we chatted and exchanged numbers. She told me that God had anointed me to be an apostle to my generation of believers. This turned out to be another divine connection which would evolve me to the next stage of my experience. She accepted me as a spiritual son and came to the With One Accord Church for a service in which I accepted the mantle of apostle. Ever since that moment, she and her administrative staff have continued to frequent Greenville to take part in the Leadership Summits with the community. She was also there when I was commissioned as an apostle.

Back in 1989, when I was initially led to receive the Lord as my one and only Savior, the minister told me, "Seek, aim at, and strive after His kingdom first of all, then His righteousness, His way of doing and being, and then all these things taken together will be given you."

For book discussions and/or signings contact the author:
Lincoln E. Anderson
La1sr@me.com

1

Made in the USA
Columbia, SC
28 May 2023